SEASONS
OF
MY HEART

RON BARTALINI

Sundie Enterprises
Since 1972

Sundie Enterprises
P.O. Box 1274
Provo, Utah 84603-1274

ISBN 978-0-9859811-7-4
Library of Congress Control Number
2016903664
Bartalini, Ron

Description: Seasons of My Heart is a poetical
record of the first animal, "Rusty," the first
butterfly, "Tony," the first object, "My beautiful
sailing ship" and the first people that touched the
author's heart and the seasons in which they
appeared.

PROLOGUE

One

I am at best
just a man
but most of all
a man.

I feel things
differently
than Linda
and my emotions
ride a different train
to towns and places
where no woman
has ever been.

Still
I travel on
and keep looking.

I've seen so many cities
it almost
seems strange
that each one
has someone
who is
a little
at best,
like
me.

Two

The days I've spent
waiting
can't be counted
or understood
by anyone
with just
a looking glass
and a hired
private eye.

It takes more
than Dick Tracy
to
understand love.

All the lonely people
who once knew love
will one day
teach
the astronomers
a proper lesson
on the higher math
of
love.

Three

There are
no set times
or seasons
for
love.

Hunting season started
yesterday
and will last
all
year
long.

You set the clocks.
You be
the
time
keeper.
And if love leaves,
you give back
the key.

Four

I must have been born
to be
a traveler
never knowing
a pair of arms
I could trust
to hold
only me
for long
and
longer.

Sometimes
I almost think
it's better
this way.

Then
as I come home again
to see old men
mowing lawns
and building
their safe
brick houses
I think
that what they have
should be a part of me.

It's what's inside
those brick houses
that we all need
but sometimes
forget.

Then Sunday morning
rolls around
and things get good again.

Sundays
were made for lovers
but most of all-
for
love.

So even if your love
isn't there
as you come home-

when Sunday
stands knocking
at your door-

Greet her
with
love.

SPRING

Rusty

I must have been
the happiest
boy in all
the world
the day I first laid eyes
on
Rusty.

If ever I knew love before
Rusty nurtured it
set a fire under my heart
and taught me how to feel
as no human
ever could.

Rusty seemed to always
be studying me
or watching out for me
even then.

Our most marvelous hours
were spent
in my childhood backyard
with our friend Tony the
butterfly
who always
managed to
come around
to help me
when I was mowing
the
backyard lawn.

I find it hard to believe
that I could come to love
a dog
I only had in my possession
for such a short time
so
deeply.

But alas
it is true
I do love Rusty
with such a great love
that my very heart
has had to stretch
out
to accommodate
my love.

Somewhere in the sky-
you can see it
on the proper night
there is a star
where Rusty
is living now.
Tony the butterfly
lives there too,
and there are
lots of children
for them
to
play with.

Surely this must
be true
for any living thing
who
loved
so completely
as Rusty did
will surely have
that love returned.

All the little children
I know
can point
to the star
where Rusty
and
Tony live.

Children understand
such things.

And somehow
because of Rusty
I will always
be a little boy
at heart
even though
I do look like
a grown-up
on
the outside.

Cuddles

What happened to you?
A little rag doll
from my childhood
before Tommy
was born
before I was two.

For awhile after that
by the looks
of
you.

Why you only have
closed
sleepy eyes
drawn on
your
cloth face.

There are now holes
in your
left leg.

Even a hole
on the top of your head
that needs
to be sown.

You don't even have
fingers
only thumbs.

But I remember
one day
on the way to
Grandma's house
when I realized
we had left you home
and I screamed
and cried
till daddy
turned the car around.

Bless his heart
for
doing that.

Thank heavens
we were only
a few blocks away!

Maybe
that's what makes
even
an inanimate
object
have value and worth.

Not the cost
of the thing
but the fact
that a child
makes their daddy
go back home
to get it
when it is forgotten.

Care worn
but not forgotten.
Tucked neatly away
by my dear mother
and now me
to have a place
in my memory
forever.

Cuddles.
My Cuddles.

Little T-Poy

Who did it?
Little T-Poy did it.

I miss little T-Poy.
Where did he go?

Grew up to be
a grown-up
like most children do.
And a fine grown-up
he is--
strong
and true.

I miss the boy
who was little T-Poy.

What a grand time
we had
in our backyard
then.
Ruled the whole neighborhood
before we were ten.

Tommy climbed up a ladder
before he was two.
I was standing at the bottom
of that ladder
so I know it's true.
Climbed all the way up
to
the
garage roof.
Wanted to help his dad
nail down new shingles
on
that roof.

Would have climbed up
to the moon
to get to his dad
if the ladder
kept on goin'.

I miss little T-Poy.
Where did he go?

One day
when I was riding my bicycle
home from school
two of my friends
rode up on their bikes
and stopped real fast.

"Tommy's in a fight
with two kids
in the sand pit
at the edge
of the school yard
and needs
to be saved."

I turned my bicycle
on a dime
and lit out lickety-split.

But when I arrived
I was surprised to find
Little T-Poy
was doing just fine.

He was winning the fight
all on
his
own.

Was I
ever proud
of Tommy
on our way back home!

I miss little T-Poy.
where did he go?

I miss Tommy
when he was a boy.

Cowboys and Indians

No kids in our neighborhood
had a chance
of invading
or conquering
the safety
of
our backyard.

When Rusty and Tony
went away
my little brother Tommy
took their place
and the first thing
we learned to do
was to become
the best cowboys
or Indians
on the block
as the situation
would demand.

I had watched enough
Saturday afternoon movies
to know the importance
of bows and arrows
and nobody could shoot up
more bad guys
With cap guns
and BB gun rifles
than we could!

We also made
the best dirt clods
in
town.
We always kept plenty on hand
with one or two rubber band
launchers at the ready
made from old worn out tire
tubes.

If that wasn't enough
I became an expert
at making adobe bricks
and digging underground
secret
escape tunnels.

We had the most impressive
fort
in town!

Then one day
I learned how
to
make a tomahawk.

That led to
our
first war.

I still carry a scar
on my hand
from an enemy arrow
but Tommy and I
won the war
and from that day on
all the kids
in the neighborhood
were on our side.

Girl Friends

One

My first girl friend's name was
Sherrie.
You may think I'm crazy
Sherrie
but I still have
the valentine
you gave me in the second
grade.

It means a lot to me.

I still remember the light blue
T-shirt with brown trim,
you gave it to me
for
my birthday.

Somehow
remembering such things
becomes more important
as one
grows older.

Girl Friends

Two

I can remember
the exact moment
you passed your love note
to
me.

Do you remember?

You wrote,
I like your actions.
Pretty big stuff
for a
third grader.

And then in the fourth grade
I defended
your honor
At your house
after
school.
It was in your driveway.

Larry and I wrestled
until I made him say,
I give.

But do you remember?

I know Larry remembers
but that doesn't seem
to be
enough.

Write and tell me
if
you do.

I would ask you
if only I knew where
to
find you.

The only things I have
to reassure me
these things are true
are
the schoolhouse
we used to attend
and
your old house
and drive way.

Heroes

One

What a day it was
when Mrs. Fish
made me read
my first book
from
cover to cover.

I salute you dear lady
for at the early age
of eight
you taught me
that books
are
the way
to
discovery.

I read all about
King Arthur
and the Knights
of the Round Table
and the magnificent
Sword *Excalibur.*

The very next day-
I made the most glorious
wooden sword
you could imagine.

Then-
Tommy and I
learned how to make
shields
out of cardboard boxes.

In no time at all
two little boys
were wonderfully transformed
into two knights
from
King Arthur's court.

Heroes

Two

When I was a child
I was the Lone Ranger.
My little brother
was
Tonto.

We'd ride together
through the streets
and alleyways
protecting
the neighbors
from bad men
and burglars
who
might creep in
and catch them unawares.

I, on my brand new
Schwinn
I code named, *Silver*
and my brother Tommy
close behind.

One afternoon
we made a campfire
in the open field
behind our grade school
but the fire got away
from us
and so we got away
from
the fire.

Sorry
grade school
alma mater-
we didn't mean
to leave your fields
all charcoal black.

Yes-
Sacramento Fire Department
the Lone Ranger
set that fire.

Carol

At twelve
I was ready for love.
at least
I thought I was.

*"Want to come to my
Barbecue?"*
I asked you.
"I'll think about it,"
You said.

"Think hard,"
I replied.

And so you did
but I can't remember
if we ever did do something
together.

Please write
and tell me
if
we did.

I only remember
your friend Vicky
and your brother Larry
and my paper route
and the seventh grade
and a barbecue
I wanted you to come to
in
my backyard.

Did

     you

          ever

               arrive?

SUMMER

FOLSOM HIGH

One

John went away for a time
when high school was done
to read college books,
smoke Winston cigarettes
in public
and feel more important.

All he ever wanted
was
$200 at one time
to buy
some
good clothes.

We had a conversation together
In 1972 or was it 1969?
I haven't seen him since.

He disappeared-
swallowed up
by the good green earth
or the time clocks
men invent.

How he loved San Francisco!
I should have taken him there.
At least taken him
some apple pie with cheese-
his favorite.

The last I heard
he was somewhere
in South America
with his own refrigerator
next to his
Air Force bed.

Is that what has become of you
John?
Mr. Myers, our high school
English
teacher who pushed the Navy
on the side
would still be proud.

I'm writing this to you now
to say I think of you
now
and then.

You
and Lake Tahoe
and
your
55 Plymouth.

And did I ever thank you
for encouraging me
to meet Georgeann
your
platonic friend?

Then did I thank you
for being
a season
of
my heart?

FOLSOM HIGH

Two

Jerry sold his Corvette
to buy a Volkswagen
and afford a wife
then it was
another wife
another Volkswagen
and finally
a little girl
and
a
new house.

But before all that
we rode through
the hills and dales
of Placer County
in his Olds 88
or my 52 Mercury
with lake pipes
and
spinner hubcaps.

Sorry I missed
our
high school
reunion.
I was away
fighting a war
or keeping another war
from
starting.

I'm not sure which anymore.

But there was a day
when Jerry and Georgeann
and I
played touch football
knee high in Folsom Lake
carefree and happy as
bluebirds
on
a
sunshine day.

FOLSOM HIGH

Three

Georgeann filled up the
daytime
with a warmth and smile
that still makes her
the most fun girl
I've ever known
and my only real
high school
sweetheart.

To me
it seems only a moment ago
that you were here
and yet
it seems
we were together
for
only
a moment.

One day
you said,
*"I'm going away
to Texas
to get married."*

And then
another season
became a faded memory.

If I had your number
or your line
I'd ring you up
to say thank you
for the season we shared
long
ago.

Meanwhile,
my heart would
smile-

If I could be sure
the season
you are living now
is happy for you.

Day of the Roses

You worked at the bakery
next door.
I worked at the grocery store.
I called you up from
a phone booth
in
the parking lot.

It was the smartest thing
I ever did as a teenager.

For the first time
the feeling I had with Rusty
was back in my heart.

Is it then true,
that you were my first love?

Is it true that I
was yours?

And so we were
young lovers.

"You have the sweetest kisses,"
you used to say.

It was not difficult for me
with someone as lovely
as
you.

Years later-
I find it almost strange
how you remember things
I had all but forgotten.

For example-
you did not
remember the hurt
you had caused me
or the why-
only the love
I brought to you.

I have learned from this
that the heart is capable
of repairing itself
from deep wounds
after many years
and each time I see you now
you remind me
of something I believe
you will never forget.

*"My husband never once
Gave me roses,"*
you told me.

And so you hang on
to the memory
of the day
I brought 16 red roses
and 16 lollipops
to your door
on
your
16th birthday.

After all these years
I am beginning now
to remember the day
of the roses
myself.

The hurt has long since
gone away.
The heart has long since
been made new.

I wonder if this
doesn't teach us
to give out love
instead
of
hurt?

And that to warm
each other's heart
is most important of all.

ANOTHER SUMMER

Remembering Mary

When I walked up behind you
on the boardwalk-
all I had
to guide me
was your
golden ponytail
glistening in the noonday sun.

I walked up along side you
looked into your eyes
and found you
to be
even more lovely
than
I had imagined.

We spent the afternoon
just talking-
lingering lazily
in
the
summer sun.

I had borrowed a guitar
and brought a friend with me.
Together we sang you
the song I had just written.

I was much too captured by
the newness of your smile
to worry about
sitting on the beach
in my street clothes
next to you
in your
bathing suit.

You were going to
spend that summer
at Meek's Bay
cleaning cabin rooms
in the morning
in order
to be able to get
a suntan
in
the afternoon.

When I told you
I was taking college classes
to graduate early-
reading, Dostoevsky
and learning about
the good green earth
you said,
"summer time is fun time."

Still-
I stayed in school
that summer and the next-
and graduated early.

Two

I drove back up to Lake Tahoe
two weeks later
to spend the weekend
with
you.

Someone
had just smashed into
the back of my cool,
customized
'56 Ford
but that wasn't going to stop
me
from
seeing you.

I arrived early in the morning
and quickly rented a motel
room.

I had come prepared
with my phonograph player
and *Rachmaninoff.*

I then drove over
to the cabin your parents
owned.
You were waiting for me
in the front yard when I
appeared.

I got out of the car
walked up to you,
took you in my arms
and kissed you softly.

Why don't
these things
happen more often
in everyone's life?

Why
do we not
realize
how close
we can come
to heaven
while we are still
alive?

We spent
a long afternoon
at the end
of your family's
private boardwalk
on the edge
of Lake Tahoe.

I'm glad I still have
a photograph
to remember
that day.

We found your favorite
Italian restaurant
that night
and lost ourselves
in the quiet-

lingering
in the flickering
candle light.

We looked deeply
into each other's eyes
and shared
our dreams.

I told you,
I wanted to write
a symphony
by the time I was 26.

You listened quietly.

You told me your dreams-
now all but forgotten
by
me.

When dinner was over–
we made our way
to the motel room
now waiting.

We spent more than an hour
in the nearby swimming pool
splashing, playing, talking
and having fun.

"Too long, too loud,"
the other guests spoke.

We finally retreated
back
to
the room.

I turned on Rachmaninoff.

We dimmed the lights
and fell away
into
forever.

Eventually
I drove you back home
at
a
respectable hour.

We said, *goodnight and adieu*
until
the morning sun
would light up
a
brand new
day.

We shared breakfast together
the
following morning.

Then I made my way down
the long and winding mountain
road
of highway 50
and back home.

Had I known then
what I know now-
I would never have
left you.

Three

My friend wanted to fly jets
for the Navy
and so for his preparation-
we rented a small plane
and flew up to Lake Tahoe
from the Nut Tree
in
California.

Before landing,
we circled Lake Tahoe
and flew over Meek's Bay.

Were you
on the beach
that day?

We should have landed on the
sandy beach.

I would have scooped you up
in my arms and flown you
to a
new star.

At least-
to a
new sky.

When we landed back home-
I should have rented a hot air
balloon
sailed back to Lake Tahoe
and landed next to you
on
the beach.

Then we could have
drifted away together
to
anywhere.

Four

Later
that summer-
I took a Greyhound bus
to Anaheim
to stay with my aunt and uncle
while I visited
an old
girl friend.

In your last letter
you said,
*"you would be working
at Disneyland that summer
and playing
Cinderella."*

I called while I was in town
but you were not there.

"Quel dommage!"

I should have called
a
hundred times.

There are not many things
in my life
I would change
if I could go back
in
time.

But this one thing I would.

I would be certain
to spend

more time

with

you.

Jordan's Song

One

I went out looking
for love again today
around the corner
and
over
the hill.

I've almost forgotten
how Jordan sings
or how good
music tasted with you.

Maybe tomorrow
will bring you
running
to my front door
with
open arms.

Oh well,
I wasn't ready
for you
today.

I still have
to watch
the apples grow
and learn
another lesson
from
the wind.

Two

When you do arrive
I'll be ready.

Going into summer
without love again
makes me wonder
if this is
the wrong time
of year
for
me.

Three

I think back
to sunshine days
in cut off Levis
walking barefoot
through the grass
and on
the
hot pavement.

Sometimes
the sand from the beach
would follow us home
and the girl
that liked me then
would send some
in her letters
that caught up to me
in
California.

Four

Where were
you
then

and what were

you
    doing?

Where

        are

           you

                now-

this

      moment?

AUTUMN

Our Own Music

You were the first
Lovely Nordic Passion girl
of
my life.

You had just come from
Denmark
to
visit Seattle.

We spent wonderful hours
driving through Sacramento
in
your red convertible
sports car-
an Austin Healey Sprite.

Working at the same store
was hard
until we could escape to
the refuge
of
your apartment.

I learned what love was
from you
and how
to
dream.

We did share
wonderful dreams
during our season-
a big house on a hill
with brick walls
and a tile roof-
remember?

I still have
the record album you gave me,
*Paul Anka, Our Man Around the
World.*
Somehow
I cannot think about you
without
hearing music.

Is
it because
there was always music
when we were together
or did we make
our
own music?

I cannot think of you without
tasting fine food
and seeing
candle light.

You brought out
the European man
in me
for
the
first time.

My, the restaurants
and quiet places
we visited in our short season!

Then
as if rehearsed
you went away-
It was Scottsdale
do you remember?

The letters came next.
two and three a week at first
then sometimes
two
a day.

I still have them
tucked neatly away.
I read one
for the first time
in years
just
the
other day.

I wonder now
how fate plays a hand
in our lives
and so I am thankful
for
our season
together.

From Sacramento to Hollywood
in such a shot time.

Do believe
I still think of you
now
and then.
Write me or ring me up
if you do too-
if just to say
hello Ronnie,
once
again.

WINTER

The Final Hour

You were the winter
of my most bitter discontent.
The only black mark
on
my heart.
A mark of sorrow
that took seven seasons
to turn white
once more.

I fully believe
that God himself
used you to teach me things
no man ever could.

You were my mother,
my father
my sister
my brother.
But never once
my lover
or friend.

I thank you for
the letters you sent
out of duty
or your concept
of
kindness.

You taught me to love
and not to love
to trust and not to trust
to believe and not to believe
to hope, and-
to give up all hope.

Though I never did.

Timing was at your option
and you waited
for the final hour
to pull
your past
out in front of me
like a gambler waits
to pull an ace
from under his sleeve
to win
a losing hand.

I winced
turned my head
backwards from the sun
gathered all your letters
one night
threw them into an empty
garbage can
marinated the can
with gasoline
and burned away
the last
memory
of you.

And yet

memories

     always

          stay-

Even
as they
     fade.

The heart can forgive

but never forget.

Walking down the highway
of my now life
I realize that you were
just a primer
expanding my heart
to hold eve more love.

I turned again into the sun.
"Thank you," I said.
I have no more bitterness
no more malcontent
only
a heart filled with
no regrets.

About the Author

Ron Bartalini was born and raised in California. He has written three other books of poetry, *"I Like You Because You Make Me Happy,"* "Whispers and Sounds" and The Continuing Story of the Lovely Nordic Passion Girl." He is also the author of *"My Greatest Love, Missionary Stories from My Life,"* "Living With and Loving All of God's Children, A Primer for Youth" Musings on manners and more and "Growing Up in America, A Primer for Youth" Musings on making your dreams come true and more. He has written two books for children, *"Hoppity Moose and the Red* Caboose" and *"The Little Leaf Tree."* He currently resides in Utah.

www.ingramcontent.com/pod-product-compliance
Lightning Source LLC
LaVergne TN
LVHW051647080426
835511LV00016B/2545